Silly RIDDLES FOR Silly KIDS

by Silly Willy

About the author

Silly Willy was born in a small town named Jill's Hills.

At the age of 6, Silly Willy moved to the top of Mount Everest to practice surfing. He failed terribly.

He now tells silly riddles to anyone who will listen.

Riddle:

What comes down but never goes up?

FIND THE ANSWER ON THE NEXT PAGE!

Answer:

Rain!

RIDDLE:

What goes up and doesn't come back down?

FIND THE ANSWER ON THE NEXT PAGE!

Answer:

Your age!

RIDDLE:

What gets wetter as it dries?

FIND THE ANSWER ON THE NEXT PAGE!

Answer:

A towel!

RIDDLE:

If two's company and three's a crowd,

what are four and five?

FIND THE ANSWER ON THE NEXT PAGE!

Answer:

9!

RIDDLE:

What gets bigger the more you take away?

FIND THE ANSWER ON THE NEXT PAGE!

Answer:

A hole!

RIDDLE:

What type of cheese is made backwards?

FIND THE ANSWER ON THE NEXT PAGE!

Answer:

Edam!

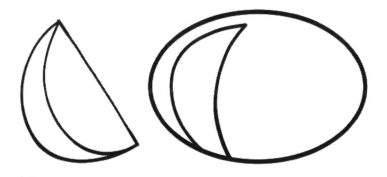

RIDDLE:

There is a rooster sitting on a top of a barn.

If it laid an egg, which way would it roll?

FIND THE ANSWER ON THE NEXT PAGE!

Answer:

Roosters don't lay eggs!

RIDDLE:

What five-letter word becomes shorter
when you add two letters to it?

FIND THE ANSWER ON THE NEXT PAGE!

Answer:

Short!

short + er

RIDDLE:

When you have me, you feel like sharing me.

If you do share me, you don't have me.

What am I?

FIND THE ANSWER ON THE NEXT PAGE!

Answer:

A secret!

RIDDLE:

A man is six feet tall, he is an assistant at the local deli and wears size nine shoes.

What does he weigh?

FIND THE ANSWER ON THE NEXT PAGE!

Answer:

Meat!

RIDDLE:

I am an odd number; take away a letter and I become even.

What number am I?

FIND THE ANSWER ON THE NEXT PAGE!

Answer:

Seven!

(SEVEN-S=EVEN)

RIDDLE:

Everyone has it and no one can lose it,
what is it?

FIND THE ANSWER ON THE NEXT PAGE!

Answer:

A shadow!

RIDDLE:

What has a face and two hands but no arms or legs?

FIND THE ANSWER ON THE NEXT PAGE!

Answer:

A clock!

RIDDLE:

What occurs twice in a week,

once in a year but never in a day?

FIND THE ANSWER ON THE NEXT PAGE!

Answer:

The letter "E"!

RIDDLE:

How many months have 28 days?

FIND THE ANSWER ON THE NEXT PAGE!

Answer:

All 12 months!

RIDDLE:

Which weighs more,

a pound of feathers or a pound of bricks??

FIND THE ANSWER ON THE NEXT PAGE!

Answer:

Neither, they both weigh one pound!

RIDDLE:

What has one eye but cannot see?

FIND THE ANSWER ON THE NEXT PAGE!

Answer:

A needle!

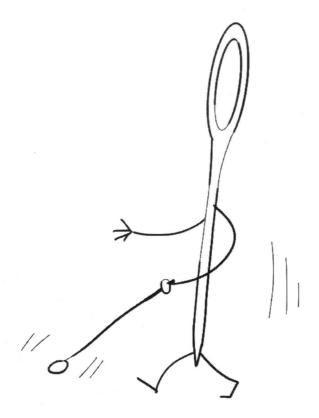

RIDDLE:

What has one head,

one foot and four legs?

FIND THE ANSWER ON THE NEXT PAGE!

Answer:

A Bed!

RIDDLE:

What is heavy forward but not backward?

FIND THE ANSWER ON THE NEXT PAGE!

Answer:

Ton!

NOT   TON

RIDDLE:

A man arrived in a small town on Friday.

He stayed for two days and left on Friday.

How is this possible?

FIND THE ANSWER ON THE NEXT PAGE!

Answer:

His horse's name is Friday!

RIDDLE:

What begins with T,

finishes with T

and has T in it?

FIND THE ANSWER ON THE NEXT PAGE!

Answer:

A teapot!

RIDDLE:

I'm tall when I'm young

and I'm short when I'm old.

What am I?

FIND THE ANSWER ON THE NEXT PAGE!

Answer:

A candle!

RIDDLE:

Poor people have it.

Rich people need it.

If you eat it you die.

What is it?

FIND THE ANSWER ON THE NEXT PAGE!

Answer:

Nothing!

RIDDLE:

What can you catch but not throw?

FIND THE ANSWER ON THE NEXT PAGE!

Answer:

A cold!

RIDDLE:

What is so fragile that saying its name breaks it?

FIND THE ANSWER ON THE NEXT PAGE!

Answer:

Silence!

RIDDLE:

You walk into a room,

it contains a match,

a kerosene lamp,

a candle,

and a fireplace.

What would you light first?

FIND THE ANSWER ON THE NEXT PAGE!

Answer:

The match!

RIDDLE:

If an electric train is travelling south,
which way is the smoke blowing?

FIND THE ANSWER
ON THE
NEXT PAGE!

Answer:

There is no smoke, it's an electric train!

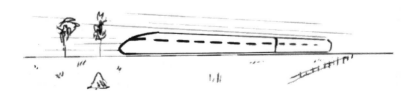

RIDDLE:

What has a neck but no head?

FIND THE ANSWER ON THE NEXT PAGE!

Answer:

A bottle!

RIDDLE:

What has to be broken before you can use it?

FIND THE ANSWER ON THE NEXT PAGE!

Answer:

An egg!

RIDDLE:

There were five people under one small umbrella.

Why didn't they get wet?

FIND THE ANSWER ON THE NEXT PAGE!

Answer:

It wasn't raining!

RIDDLE:

What has four wheels and flies?

FIND THE ANSWER ON THE NEXT PAGE!

Answer:

A garbage truck!

RIDDLE:

What is at the end of a rainbow?

FIND THE ANSWER ON THE NEXT PAGE!

Answer:

The letter W!

RIDDLE:

What travels around the world but stays in one spot?

FIND THE ANSWER ON THE NEXT PAGE!

Answer:

A stamp!

RIDDLE:

How many letters are there in the English alphabet?

FIND THE ANSWER ON THE NEXT PAGE!

Answer:

There are 18!

Three in 'the', seven in 'English' and eight in 'alphabet'.

The English Alphabet
1 2 3 4 5 6 7 8 9 10 11 12 13 14 15 16 17 18

RIDDLE:

I am the beginning of the end,

and the end of time and space.

I surround every place.

What am I?

FIND THE ANSWER ON THE NEXT PAGE!

Answer:

The letter 'E'!

End, timE, spacE, Every placE!

RIDDLE:

What is the longest word in the dictionary?

FIND THE ANSWER ON THE NEXT PAGE!

Answer:

Smiles!

There is a <u>mile</u> between each 's'!

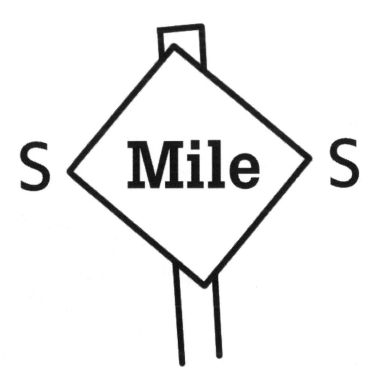

RIDDLE:

If a red house is made out of red bricks,

and a yellow house is made out of yellow bricks,

what is a green house made of??

FIND THE ANSWER ON THE NEXT PAGE!

Answer:

Glass!

RIDDLE:

What is always coming but never arrives?

FIND THE ANSWER ON THE NEXT PAGE!

Answer:

Tomorrow!

RIDDLE:

What has 88 keys,

but cannot open a single door?

FIND THE ANSWER ON THE NEXT PAGE!

Answer:

A piano!

RIDDLE:

What has a bed but never sleeps,

can run but never walks,

and has a bank but no money?

FIND THE ANSWER ON THE NEXT PAGE!

Answer:

A river!

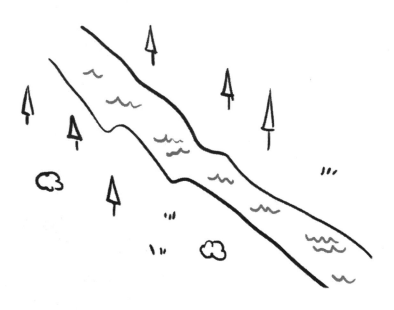

RIDDLE:

Can you name two days starting with T,

besides Tuesday and Thursday?

FIND THE ANSWER ON THE NEXT PAGE!

Answer:

Today and tomorrow!

RIDDLE:

What is the center of Gravity?

FIND THE ANSWER ON THE NEXT PAGE!

Answer:

The letter V!

RIDDLE:

What kind of room has no doors or windows?

FIND THE ANSWER ON THE NEXT PAGE!

Answer:

A mush-room!

RIDDLE:

I have keys but no locks.

I have space but no room.

You can enter but can't go outside.

What am I?

FIND THE ANSWER ON THE NEXT PAGE!

Answer:

A Keyboard!

RIDDLE:

What can you hold without using your hands?

FIND THE ANSWER ON THE NEXT PAGE!

Answer:

Your breath!

RIDDLE:

The more of them you take,

the more you leave behind.

What are they?

FIND THE ANSWER ON THE NEXT PAGE!

Answer:

Footsteps!

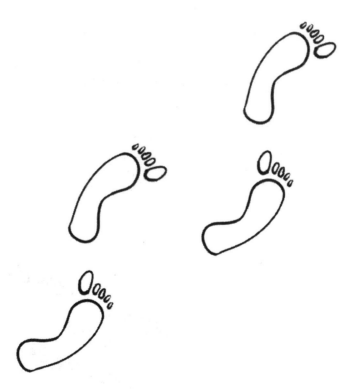

RIDDLE:

What is full of holes,

but still holds water?

FIND THE ANSWER ON THE NEXT PAGE!

Answer:

A sponge!

RIDDLE:

What word in the English language is always spelt incorrectly?

FIND THE ANSWER ON THE NEXT PAGE!

Answer:

Incorrectly!

RIDDLE:

Who can shave 25 times a day and still have a beard?

FIND THE ANSWER ON THE NEXT PAGE!

Answer:

A Barber!

RIDDLE:

What is the tallest building in town?

FIND THE ANSWER ON THE NEXT PAGE!

Answer:

The library (it has a lot of stories)!

RIDDLE:

The one who made it, didn't want it.

The one who bought it, didn't need it.

The one who used it, never saw it.

What is it?

FIND THE ANSWER ON THE NEXT PAGE!

Answer:

A coffin!

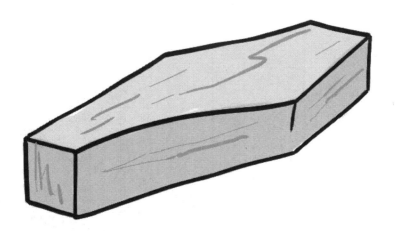

RIDDLE:

If a cow eats 10 pounds of grass,

how much milk should it drink?

FIND THE ANSWER ON THE NEXT PAGE!

Answer:

Cows don't drink milk, they drink water!

RIDDLE:

What do you call a boomerang that does not work?

FIND THE ANSWER ON THE NEXT PAGE!

Answer:

A stick!

RIDDLE:

A man turned out all the lights and went to bed.

He woke up realizing that he made a mistake.

Where did the man live?

FIND THE ANSWER ON THE NEXT PAGE!

Answer:

He lived in a light house!

RIDDLE:

What needs an answer,

but doesn't ask a question?

FIND THE ANSWER ON THE NEXT PAGE!

Answer:

A telephone!

RIDDLE:

I have no life,

but I can die.

What am I?

FIND THE ANSWER ON THE NEXT PAGE!

Answer:

A battery!

RIDDLE:

What kind of key opens a banana?

FIND THE ANSWER ON THE NEXT PAGE!

Answer:

A monkey!

RIDDLE:

What's taken before you get it?

FIND THE ANSWER ON THE NEXT PAGE!

Answer:

Your picture!

RIDDLE:

What's black and white and red all over?

FIND THE ANSWER ON THE NEXT PAGE!

Answer:

A newspaper!

RIDDLE:

What has a bottom at the top?

FIND THE ANSWER ON THE NEXT PAGE!

Answer:

Your legs!

RIDDLE:

Where does Friday come before Monday?

FIND THE ANSWER ON THE NEXT PAGE!

Answer:

In the dictionary!

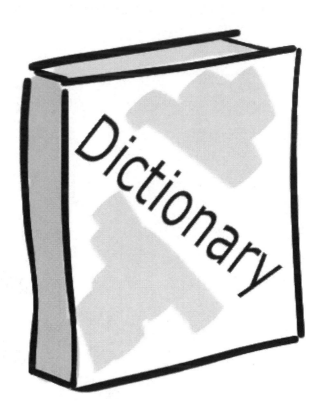

RIDDLE:

What can you put in a barrel to make it lighter?

FIND THE ANSWER ON THE NEXT PAGE!

Answer:

Holes!

The End

Also Available:

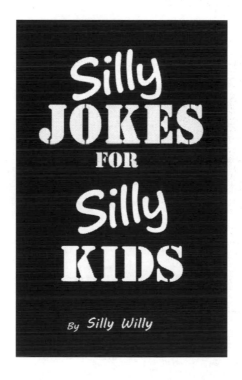

77616303R00071

Made in the USA
Middletown, DE
23 June 2018